Rag Manifesto

making, folklore & community

Rachael Matthews

'The fairest order in the world is a heap of random sweepings.'

Heraclitus, Fragments, *c. 500BC*

QUICKTHORN

Rag Manifesto
© 2024 Rachael Matthews

Published by Quickthorn
info@quickthornbooks.com
www.quickthornbooks.com
@quickthornbooks

Editor: Katy Bevan
Cover: Shoulder Boulder, Rachael Matthews
Cover photo: Antranig Basman
Cover design: Adams Associates
Book design and typesetting: Chris J Bailey
Printed in the UK by Cambrian

Printed on uncoated FSC certified paper

British Library Cataloguing
in Publication Data applied for
ISBN 978-1-7393160-3-7

Contents

Rag DNA
This is my DNA in felted and darned cable knit.

Intelligent rag
Based on an ancient symbol for intelligence
in motion, made with Kumihimo braid in rag.

living crisis, many families cannot provide such cupboards of opportunity. Materials continue to provide this support structure for me, teaching me new skills and making me think about where I do, and don't, belong.

The random ways rags reach us, leads to ways of working which are nearly always experimental. This open mindset is being largely lost over a few generations of capitalism, where all products or instructive patterns are designed to deliver clearly understood objects of desire.

Some rag projects can be instantly successful, while others can wait ages for something else to come into view. Unproven aesthetics can lead us to doubt ourselves as artists and designers. The preliminary nature of mixing rags often requires a generous dose of time to consider what it is that is emerging. Don't lose heart and keep a curiosity box full of your unresolved experiments. Fate might deliver you the perfect fabric some time hence. Discuss these problems openly with your friends. Even Picasso found that some of his works endured a long, hard, journey towards the limelight.

The ideas we uncover as we work with rags may be successful now, or they may only become significant later; it really doesn't matter which so long as you are making things with some sort of rebellion in mind. Some of the things you make may simply be waiting it out until they become relevant and your thinking has developed enough to tackle them.

I want to share an affirmation by the artist Yoko Ono*, which gets me started in the mornings, or clears my head of worries in the evenings.

Thank you thank you thank you
Thank you for the beautiful
Planet we live on and enjoy,
In the most interesting, exciting and
Enlightening time in the history
Of the human race.
Each of us was born at this time
To fulfil a mission.
Together we are in a process of healing
And creating a better world
For the lives of the planet
Our work is not yet done,
But it will be done soon.

Rachael Matthews

✱ As heard on BBC Radio 4, 'Oh Yoko', 12th May 2023 to mark Yoko Ono's 90th birthday. Produced by Mae-Li Evans.

rag manifesto

Ancient Ways

Relearning ways of making things

'The idea that a culture could reveal more of itself through its throwaway items than through its supposedly revered artifacts was fascinating to me. Still is.'

Jarvis Cocker

Textile makers have been conscious of circular design since the beginning of time. Ancient cultures took fibres from animals and plants, working them with devotion and skill. In return, the materials protected them, bringing loveliness to a few generations of folk before disintegrating back into the earth as a nutritious fertiliser. It was a simple system, overflowing with human genius.

In more recent textile history, something weird happened. Economic growth found a way to exploit the special human attraction to vibrating patterns, twinkly things, iridescence, and pseudo soft touches. Clever synthetic tricks created wild, transcending desires which made us lose our way.

The famous textile designer and social activist, William Morris referred to these desires as 'shamwants' – things you think you want but of which you soon tire. We are led to believe that buying things and then quickly abandoning them is a good intellectual choice, but it causes many people to lose touch with nature. In the textile world, shamwants begat through fast fashion and the manipulation of people on low incomes, cause excess fabrics to be shifted around the planet in huge containers, unsure of their destination, resold again and again and often ending up in landfill.

When our clothes come to us, they arrive at the end of a very long series of processes. Fibres are beaten, raked, washed, brushed, baked; dye powders are ground or sliced; acids are mixed. Next comes spinning, plying, skeining, rewashing, followed by mordanting, dying, washing again, drying, steaming, ball winding, weighing, labelling, weaving, fulling, finishing, more steaming and rolling. Then there is cutting and tacking; the stitching of seams and the top stitching of seams; lining, detailing, pressing, altering and quality control followed by packaging, shipping, unpacking, displaying and selling.

Shamwant 1
Shiny and totally useless,
William Morris described
'shamwants' as things you
may think you want but of
which you will soon tire.

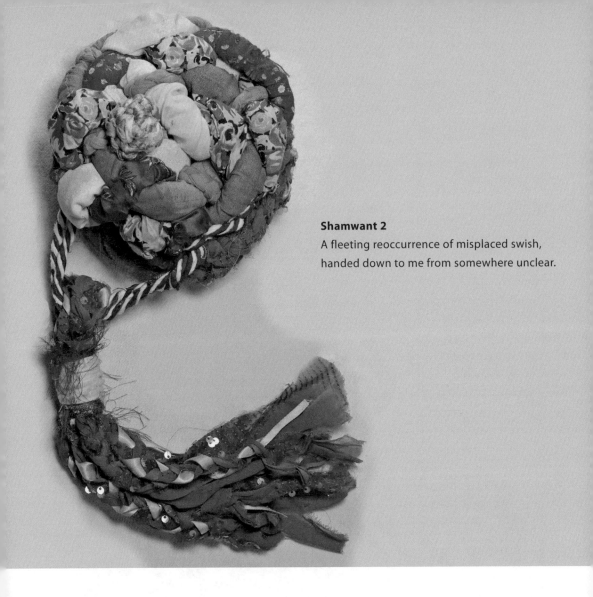

Shamwant 2
A fleeting reoccurrence of misplaced swish,
handed down to me from somewhere unclear.

But thinking through this huge list of textile-making processes gives us an opportunity to join a long and skilled dynasty, inherent in every problematic piece of clothing. The action of chopping to make rag yarn is just the next stage.

There are processes for everyone to enjoy, they just need searching out. Crafts people tend to be willing to pass on their cultural heritage and teach you what they know; all you have to do is ask. (Watching the working hands of the committed people giving free tuition on the internet will speak to you too.)

I want to work with the lessons of ancient civilisations, combined with nature, to ensure that we leave surfaces as beautiful as the geology and fossils we love to collect.

Rag School

Rag School

'Most learning is not the result of instruction. It is rather the result of unhampered participation in a meaningful setting.'

Ivan Illich, *Deschooling Society*

During the Covid-19 lockdowns, I would take my family to our local park in London for our daily exercise. We kept walking past heaps of clothes and household fabrics lying in the streets. Reduced waste collection services, combined with people having time to clear out their cupboards, showed very clearly just how much textile waste the average person was capable of making.

Touching anything alien during a pandemic was considered dangerous, but as I was masked and gloved and in possession of a wheelbarrow, I took action. I pushed the first load home and, after running it through a 90-degree wash cycle, I was astonished to find full spectrums of colour emerging from my washing machine. With the charity shop closed indefinitely, I chopped the garments into yarn and re-learned weaving.

Once I was walking down our street with a wheelbarrow full of old curtains and a lady stopped her car, wound down her window and said, 'Excuse me! I've seen you before and I have no idea what you are doing but thank you for doing it.' And then she drove off.

Around the same time, I heard about a lockdown studio project called 'What to do today?' run by Diane Haigh, a professor of architecture at Cambridge University. Diane's vision was that Zoom could be a place where people worked in virtual studios and

Free for all

Instagram poster made during Covid-19 lockdown for the first wave of Rag School as part of Prof. Diane Haigh's 'What to do today?' online programme of re-thinking workshops.

Bunting

Thank you to the first wave rag schoolers for letting me make bunting out of these screenshots by Sallyanne Wood. It is appreciated that Facetime software doesn't always enhance complexions, or well-considered colour senses, but I'm sure you will agree we all look beautiful!

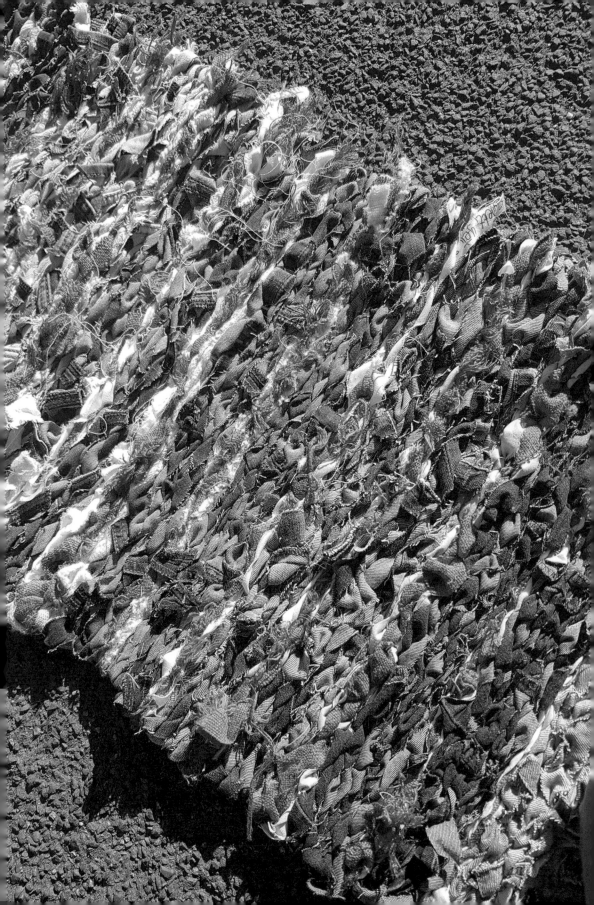

Virtual Rag Studio
Rag Studio was founded
online during lockdown
with Diane Haigh, and
was a series of online
events. I was working
with families in the park
at that time, and that
generated ideas which
fed back into the studio.
It became known by
participants as Rag
School. Post lockdown
I joined East London
Textile Arts (ELTA)
and it became 'Rag
School at ELTA'.

trialled new ways of teaching, learning and
forming communities. I wrote to Diane
suggesting I set up a virtual rag studio and
she immediately encouraged the idea.

Our open call for participants through social
media gathered a diverse group of 12 people
spanning several time zones and professions.
To begin with, I invited visiting speakers to
inspire us and used my teaching experience
to make sure that all the voices in the group
were heard, but pretty soon the Rag Studio
was happy and needed no steering. The online
Rag Studio became a space for sharing
indigenous skills, experimenting, having a
laugh and showing off high-quality work,
demonstrating that banked knowledge
gushes out if you ask it to.

Rich pickings
My wheelbarrow of joy blocking the hall.

Sari Pompoms
Philippa Brock.
Photo Andrew Brown.

Rachael
Teaching at ELTA.
Photo by Sameena.

Black and White Rubble
Made with Welsh
weaving sticks.
(Detail, see p102.)

Backstrap loom

Backstrap loom weaving is quite easy once you get strapped in. Traditionally, backstrap looms are used sitting on the floor with one end of the warp threads attached to a tree or a fence and the other end attached to you, via a stick and a belt. A simple heddle moves the warp threads up and down. Your body creates the tension as you lean back into the work, stretching your hamstrings at the same time.

Backstrap loom
Here is a variation demonstrated on the public cycling machine. I prefer this method in winter because it keeps you warm and fit. Photo Antranig Basman.

Tent peg rug

This technique is adapted from a knitting loom method where pegs on four sides of a square hold multiple warp threads worked up and down and left to right. Traditionally, a crochet hook can be used to make loops through the intersecting warp threads, forming a granny square, or you can tie lots of little knots where the warp threads meet.

Tent peg rug
This rug was made with the tent peg method. It started its life beige but somehow I lost heart, so I dyed it green. The green worked much better for me working outside because it matched the grass. Perhaps if I did this technique on the beach, I would go back to beige. Anyway, the ties were all multi-coloured to represent the seeds we planted that summer and which didn't grow.

Working by a lake in the park, I replaced the loom and pegs with tent pegs hammered into soft ground. Tent pegs are tall and allow you to make your warp quite thick and any overall dimension. Load the warp up, down and side to side with rag. Where your warp and weft threads cross over, secure with a knot, bow or crochet embellishment The knots on this piece are from a silver blouse and the warp threads come from a Jacquard-woven upholstery fabric. Here is Magnus, helping to turn the weave into a foot stool that is light enough to carry to the park for other Rag School adventures.

The weaving started as fun, practical action, but then a commission came to ELTA to work on a project with Dr Rachel Scott from Royal Holloway, University of London on 'Kalila Wa Dimla', an ancient tale of four friends: a deer, crow, rat and turtle.

This carpet represents the deer, and has a big zip so that you can actually wear it like a cape. The main weave was made in three strips on a simple 18 inch Brinkley Loom, which fits perfectly on the picnic table.

The weaves were put through a brown dye bath to create the effect of deer skin. Once dry, we embellished it with the words, in high-vis rags:

> 'Deer don't cross the road;
> the road crosses the forest.'

Tent peg rug
The loom was created with tent pegs hammered into the ground and allowed many hands to contribute.

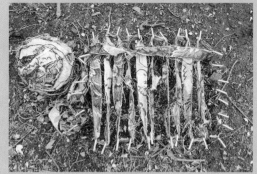

All wrapped up

Here is Sallyanne wrapped in a blanket made by our community at ELTA. This piece was made entirely out of fabric from the park and its surrounding streets. Sometimes the community can fill your head with so many questions that the best thing to do is wrap yourself up in a carpet the community has made, go to sleep and let the mind work its magic. Photo Andrew Brown for East London Textile Arts.

rag manifesto

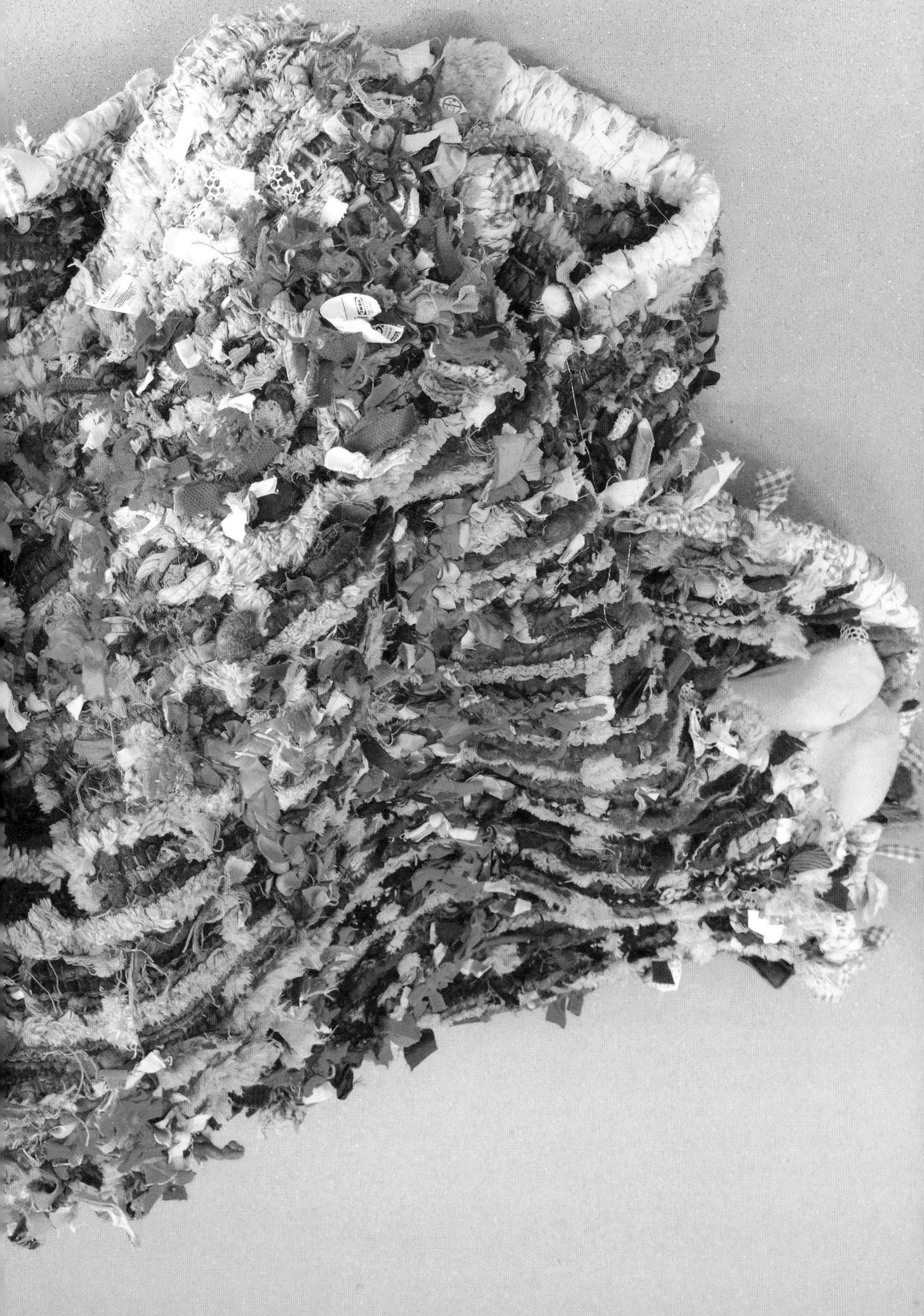

Deer don't cross the road
Made by East London Textile Arts members for
the Kalila Wa Dimna, Ancient Tales for Troubled
Times project. Photo Andrew Brown.

East London Textile Arts

Weaving with ELTA

'All weaving is the interlacing of two distinct groups of threads at right angles.'

Anni Albers, *On Weaving*

Let me introduce you to the work of East London Textile Arts (ELTA) where I am a studio leader along with embroiderer and community textile tutor Sonia Tuttiett. ELTA is an independent collective running participatory textile projects.

We work with diverse groups of all abilities on a long-term developmental basis, building a wide range of skills within the community. We create striking artworks and have a range of merchandise. We also work with adults with learning disabilities and collaborate with visiting artists while training unemployed young people.

Feet rooted in our local context Photo Andrew Brown.

Rag River Roding

Photos by Andrew Brown for
the River Roding Trust.

Rag River Roding
Ryan Powell's Sensory Attunement Coracle.
Photo Andrew Brown, River Roding Trust.

On the move
Peace signs on the river.
Photo Rachael Matthews.

As the Covid-19 lockdowns eased, I was commissioned by ELTA to start a rag weaving studio in a newly built school in Newham. The school was part of a large-scale redevelopment of an old industrial area down by the river and our job was to make community art so, Rag Studio became Rag School.

Joining ELTA gave me room to establish a real-life studio within an existing funding structure, while giving ELTA new reasons to source funding. Rag School collaborates with many other projects and institutions, but ELTA provides it with a sense of mothership. Artists who run community projects are often in danger of identity crisis because they must identify as a whole community, therefore forfeiting their name. ELTA's craftivism rolls for a greater good, with our individual and collective identities engaged in the textile ether. The ELTA website has good advice on how to run a community textile project.

The school, which only had its first year's intake, gave us an empty classroom in which to work and we gratefully received a Community Lottery Grant to make workshops. Textile enthusiasts can always be counted upon and after a few weeks of outreach work, brave pioneers appeared on a regular basis and we got busy. I am very grateful to our rag weavers for the wonderful story they generated for this book.

Figuring out how a Rag School could form in other communities is hard to speculate as diverse communities and places are all so unique. What I must emphasise is that we were lucky to be hosted by a school which gave us a big enough space in which to pile up the rag. Permanent space with permission to make a mess is the key to starting a community rag project.

As we were setting up the Rag School, an introduction to a neighbouring community led to our first site-specific project. The River

Rag in the City
Sandra, Sallyanne and Sindy carry our Rag River weave all the way to the City of London for an Exhibition. Photo Sameena.

Roding runs from Stansted Airport all the way down to the River Thames. It has many fascinating ancient histories, but, in modern times, it became hemmed in by industrial infrastructure. Parts of the river were heavily polluted by factories and concrete jungles were built hard up to its edge. Finding peace for contemplation near water should be a human right, especially in the city, and yet this waterway was being ruined by a fast turnover of drug dens and fly tipping. Among all this rubbish was an alarming quantity of discarded textiles.

The River Roding Trust was formed by a group of house boaters and environmentalists who wanted to restore and protect the river and its natural habitats. In 2021, ELTA won a National Lottery Community Grant to make a textile exhibition 'Adventures on the River Roding', drawing attention to this environmental work. Helping with the Sunday afternoon litter picks, aided by the Trust's shopping trolley boombox, we took

inspiration from the restored waters, flourishing reed beds, birds nesting on handbuilt rafts and kingfishers flashing past the neighbouring motorway.

Just as nature responded swiftly to the Trust's actions, the transformation of waste fabric into Rag River Rugs also happened quickly. Peg looms and Welsh weaving sticks are simple to use, and our community came together to prepare the materials. We studied the colours on the waterways and in the urban environment too as graffiti and tower blocks are important parts of this landscape.

Participants who felt shy about making creative decisions found the physical exercise of ripping cloth a good way to find states of flow. Conversations about colour are not intellectual and are often non-verbal, involving grunts, sighs, silences, gasps of excitement, waving of arms, hugs or even dancing with combinations of rag in hand.

As a facilitator, I learned to lay aside personal visions of the finished product and let faith in people take over. Materials in the hands, a shared love of nature and perhaps, in some cases, a shared love of God, work as guiding forces in collaborative design. Unexplainable and deeply sustainable, all I can say is that when people's energies combine in the work, enchanting things can happen.

Some participants found my intermittent withdrawal of instruction difficult, especially if they were worrying about letting the group down in its collaborative work. I would rather see an authentic response to colour than have everyone follow my vision. Strange and worrying combinations of colour and texture did happen of course, and some of them caused people to have sleepless nights, but inclusion was the key; unpicking or throwing away 'wrong' work were the only things I didn't allow. The strangeness of trying something new became integral to the brilliance. Cycles of reflection and action brought more care to the work. The river was also changing as a result of care. We were all in it together.

When our River Rugs were finished, we wanted to take them to the river for a photo shoot. On the first clear day of early summer, sunglasses on, we took our massively heavy rugs on the riverboat, journeying up the Thames from north Greenwich to the Tower of London, to make a presentation to the professional weavers at The Experimental Weave Lab* at the Clothworker's Company. On our journey we posed for photos with our work.

Entering the Lab, I could sense a communal relief as we committed amateur weavers found ourselves in the company of professionals who respected our work and our collaborative design story. Our hosts were intrigued to hear how our Rag Rivers came into being and the Lab residents' work, displayed on the walls and looms, invited us to share a common language, boosting our passions for future projects. This day trip up the Thames with our work brought us inspiration for new ways of working. We realised that, as Kate Fletcher and Mathilda Tham wrote in 'Earth Logic', our 'decisions are made on the go with robustness arising from rootedness in local context'.

Both the River Roding Trust and Experimental Weave Lab invited us into a 'don't know space' resulting in a rich melting

* The Experimental Weave Lab was founded by Philippa Brock and Elizabeth Ashdown in 2022 and I was a resident weaver there, along with eight others. The Experimental Weave Lab aims to explore the interstitial spaces that weavers work within throughout UK craft, research, art, design and industry. The Experimental Weave Lab curated a special programme of events for London Craft Week 2022 celebrating the rare and endangered craft of Passementerie.

Weaving stick mat

Throughout the project we dreamed of our work floating on the river, taking us with it. A few months later we met Ryan Powell with his Sensory Attunement Coracle, a sculpture he made as an offering to the River Roding. One of our rugs fit perfectly within it.

You can see Ryan's film on YouTube. Photos Antranig Basman.

Let your fabrics
rest in peace and
rise in power

R.I.P.

Rip – 1. tear or pull (something) quickly or forcibly away from something or someone.
2. Move forcefully and rapidly

Oxford English Dictionary

The 'split' second when you cut or rip cloth can be exhilarating. Once it is done, it is done, so allow yourself to be transported through a ceremonial moment as there is no way back. I like to rip and cut as ritual, enjoying the sounds of destruction and winding the yarn into neat balls, ready to display as my riches.

Ripping makes dust. Wear a mask and have your vacuum cleaner ready. If the fabric is natural, ripping outside is great. If you suspect synthetic content in the material, take extra care over straying fibres.

Good fabric scissors are a great investment for rag work. Never let anyone use your fabric scissors for cutting paper and cards; it blunts them. Non-textile people never understand this, so guard your tools. Pinking shears enable you to chop without fray. I really dig the fray, but sometimes the edges need to have a good, clean zig zag. To rip with more frenzy, you could investigate rotary cutters, some of which are electric. Electric blades freak me out, so I will just say please concentrate. Overuse of scissors can hurt your hands and all repetitive work should be complemented with body stretches.

Cat on a mat
Our cat likes to sit on anything that I am in the middle of making.

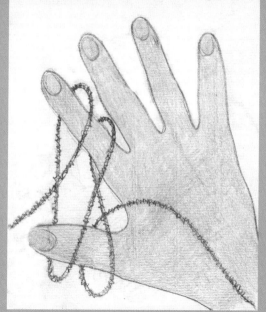

1 Begin by winding the yarn around your thumb and first finger

4 …and start winding it like this.

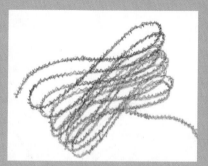

2 Making a figure of 8 foundation like this.

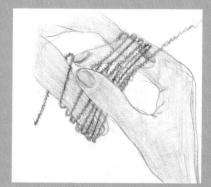

3 Now you need to fold this bundle in half…

This traditional way of winding yarn into a ball allows you to pull the thread from the centre.

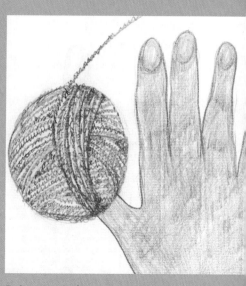

5 As you wind, you can use your thumb to hold the bundle, wrapping round and round until it becomes a ball. The ball can turn around the thumb, and the yarn can spiral as you go!

Perfect your technique by watching online demonstrations. Scandinavians use a nostepinne instead of a thumb. Putting the love into ball winding gives your display of materials an extra certain something.

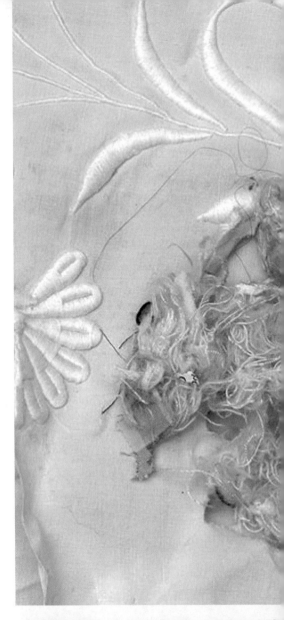

When a ball of rag yarn appears, it will sit there like a strange planet, exuding an intelligence that it didn't show in its previous life. There might be a hidden meaning underneath its surface. Ideas about its destiny might be obvious, or it could sit on the shelf for a while. The singer-songwriter Patti Smith describes this organic way of working beautifully in her memoir *Year of the Monkey*. The back cover of the book says, 'Unfettered by logic or time, she draws us into her private wonderland with no design, yet heeding signs.' So we attend to the signals that the materials send us and wait to hear what they tell us.

Creative usess of rag yarn crosspollinate cultures and species. My husband sees textiles relating to nature, my son relates them to his building of robots, but horses, cats and dogs, birds, rodents, or any other creature you share your space with, could give you a sense of how the yarn wants to live. Our cat makes territorial moves on anything I am making, while my friend's dog thinks every ball of yarn is a game for her. These animals arrive as work starts, while others get busy when we have gone to bed.

Pokey rugs made by humans from tiny scraps have a similar feel to mouse work, but could never be so tender. Mice teach us that the smallest of fragments can be very important. The bits that are too small to do anything with can be destined for something else, such as a nest or the lettering for the cover of this book.

Human Pokey Pokey rugs made by humans from tiny scraps have a similar feel to mouse work.

Mouse house

This is work made by a house mouse, mus musculus, who moved into the top drawer of my mother's 18th century tallboy chest, a safe place to bring up a family away from predators and a pleasure garden of fabric in which to build a home. The mouse masterpiece is made from a fancy handmade 19th century lace tablecloth and a perfectly faded red gingham curtain from the 1950s. The original mus musculus has left, so I replaced her with a needle felted dormouse by Karin Celestine, founder of Celestine and the Hare. Karin creates worlds where kindness, mischief and beauty help people find magic in the ordinary.

Fly Fringe
An eighteenth-century idea for
braid made from the smallest
pieces of textile waste.

In his book *The Right Way to Flourish*, John
Ehrenfeld offers an aspirational definition of
sustainability: 'the possibility that humans
and other life will flourish on Earth forever'.

Transform or die

Fashion designer Vivienne Westwood used
the phrase 'transform or die' as an
instruction for creating peace.
Transformation, as opposed to death, offers a
moment's rest after a considerable effort.

When writer and playwright Oscar Wilde
uttered his last words in Room 16 of the
Hôtel d'Alsace in Paris, he said:
*'My wallpaper and I are fighting a duel to the
death. One or the other of us must go.'*

A black and white photograph shows Oscar
surrounded by walls wrapped in a print of
cascading posies of flowers. There is
relatively strong evidence that there were
also matching drapes. Oscar's joke gives
a comical, subversive power to bad design.
He knew it was time to

'transform or die' and so he died.
To have swiped those drapes for making art,
would have proved Oscar's other famous
quote that 'ordinary riches can be stolen, real
riches cannot' to be true. In ripping up the
chintz, who knows what richness the weaves
could have had?

A decade before Oscar's duel, Charlotte
Perkins Gilman's short story, 'The Yellow
Wallpaper' told of an even darker side of
poor design. A young woman descends into
psychosis, breaking down in tune with an
unnerving repeat pattern on the walls of her
room. The pattern is unclear because it keeps
moving. Her husband, who is also her doctor,
denies her request to change rooms. The
story questions the roles of women, their
right to autonomy, good mental health and
self-identity.

Had this poor lady been able to rip the yellow
pattern into strips, might she have felt
better? Torn up, woven and placed on a floor,
this ghastly yellow pattern could have
become a rug depicting a glorious sunrise.

Sentimentality

The artist Louise Bourgeois based much of her work on the deeply psychological relationships we can develop with the textiles around us. In his book *What Artists Wear*, the fashion journalist Charlie Porter uncovered the extent to which Bourgeois went to preserve her clothes and everything that they represent. Porter translated her explanation: *'Like a dumbo, I think I am going to cry – my garments and especially my undergarments have always been a source of intolerable suffering because they hide an intolerable wound. (...) I cannot separate myself from my clothes... my past, as rotten as it was, I would like to take it and hold it in my arms.'*

Drawing on emotional intimacy with garments, Louise Bourgeois preserves a language we could become increasingly unfamiliar with as ours; demoted garments get thrown away in fits of shame, or sadness about the past. But isn't there something just as life affirming about these 'sad' fabrics as those we kept for the happy memories they hold? Wounds of

Jam jar
As creatures on planet earth, collecting bits and bobs is in our nature. Store these precious little things in jam jars until you need them for Fly Fringe. I must credit my mother-in-law Metzmama for this particular jar of bits. I wish I knew from where they flew.

the past are a reminder that we live on and weaving these intimate rags, perhaps dying them a different colour, can help us enshroud the emotion and trauma that hides in textiles. Let a memory become a woven stripe, representing parts of your personal myth.

Non-intentional rips are devastating and appear on my rag pile frequently, making me stop in my tracks wanting to mend, reverse, patch and make it good again. If a garment provides us with confidence for years, a quick little rip signals the beginning of the end. Perfect second skin ripped can feel like a catastrophe. Our 'craft of use' makes the story of the clothes we wear all the more special. As the cloth ages, fragility becomes entwined with identity.

John G Neihardt's *Black Elk Speaks: Being the life story of a holy man of the Oglala Sioux*, relays a tale from Neihardt's friend,

Fire Thunder describing an attack on their tribe by the Wasichus, or White Man. He writes, '*...they shot faster than they had ever shot at us before. We thought it was some new medicine of great power that they had, for they shot so fast that it was like a tearing blanket. Afterwards I learned that it was because they had new guns.*'

A blanket tear being used as an analogy to describe violent gunfire shows how much respect there was for essential materials. The blanket screams with a quick and devastating rip, marking the beginning of the end of its life. Materials came from the earth and no life is considered cheap in Oglala Sioux society.

Turning the rag pile into 'clues'

In the English North country, from where I come, a ball of yarn was not, historically, a ball, it was a 'clue'. Clues hung from a hook on your belt so that you could knit as you walked to market, wandered across the fields or wherever else your busy life led you. Word has it that a knitter could unravel their yarn on a journey to give a clue as to how to get home in a fog. There must be truth in this, but I also know that the action of sitting with a ball of yarn in your hands presents you with many clues as to how the material can evolve into something, and how the process of evolving the material and the arrival of that physical thing, might change all sorts of other, more abstract things.

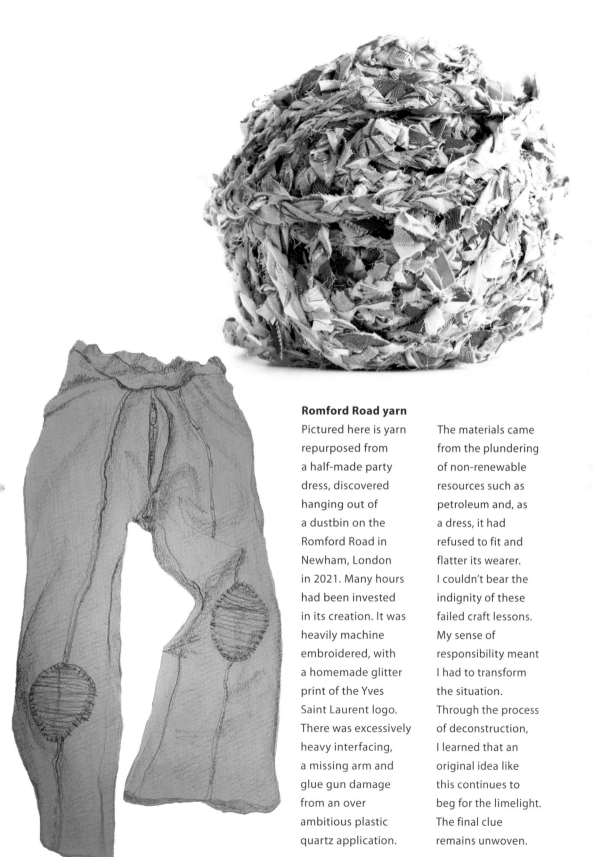

Romford Road yarn

Pictured here is yarn repurposed from a half-made party dress, discovered hanging out of a dustbin on the Romford Road in Newham, London in 2021. Many hours had been invested in its creation. It was heavily machine embroidered, with a homemade glitter print of the Yves Saint Laurent logo. There was excessively heavy interfacing, a missing arm and glue gun damage from an over ambitious plastic quartz application.

The materials came from the plundering of non-renewable resources such as petroleum and, as a dress, it had refused to fit and flatter its wearer. I couldn't bear the indignity of these failed craft lessons. My sense of responsibility meant I had to transform the situation. Through the process of deconstruction, I learned that an original idea like this continues to beg for the limelight. The final clue remains unwoven.

53

Clues

Here is my archive of clues. Building a collection of rag yarns is the same thing as topping up a paint box. Colours come and colours go as you work. The relationships between rag yarns are always in flux as our sources are often finite and unpredictable. Attempting to arrange yarns in a rainbow formation or specific colour story will entice you to your local charity shop to add to what you have, and in turn, the charity shop will guide you into a whole new area of thought.

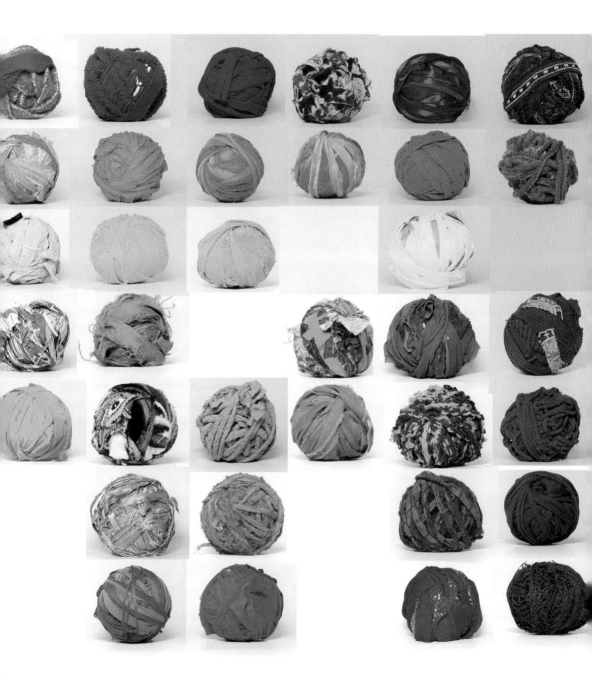

Mountains

In the English Lake District, tourists have been coming to marvel at the scenery since the late 18th century. Before the tourists arrived, the mountains were considered wild and desolate places, full of monsters and strange spirits who didn't welcome the trespassing of commoners. The attitudes to this landscape were similar to our community's view of the rag piles, which mount upon the corner of our road. Abrupt house clearance holds a weird spirit and lowers the tone of the area.

In 1724, the writer Daniel Defoe described the Lake Country as 'the wildest, most barren and frightful of any that I have passed over in England'. Another traveller suggested it was 'nothing but hideous, hanging hills' and 'a confused mixture of rocks and bogs'. Visitors to my studio with its mountains of rag in all corners could be forgiven for making the same associations.

These 18th-century travellers recognised the Lake District as a challenging place to live, with little opportunity for arable farming, frequent natural disasters and a staggering amount of work required simply to survive. Even in the 21st century, I can confirm the Lake District is a place where your clothes could wear out quickly.

The scale of the Lake District fells beckons adventurers to climb, just as the rag piles invite creatives to dig. I know I am alive if I have conquered a mountain, and I want to use that same feeling of endurance in the transformation of discarded materials. Gaining personal strength from these experiences works even better if the two activities sublimely collide. I understand attitudes to the global rag pile of the 21st century in a similar way that a 16th- or 17th-century traveller would understand the Lake Country. It is frightful indeed, but there is something to gain. I want to instigate a change in the way we see our wasted textile landscape.

In the second half of the 18th century, something changed in the way people saw mountains. The Napoleonic wars put a stop to the English travelling to Europe for the Grand Tour, so they started to search for new experiences nearer to home. Looking for splendour, awe and sublimity, they found it in the rugged mountains, dark forests and dangerous waterfalls. Beauty was perceived in the flowers, saplings, graceful pasture and light. Through witnessing the sweetness of the beautiful, mixed with the majestic terror of the sublime, the Picturesque Movement was born. Can you imagine a time coming where we develop a similar splendour towards the landscape of abundant materials all around us?

18th-century tourists started to look at landscape as if it was art, aided by the curious tool of the Claude Glass mirror, a piece of brownish/blackish mirror kept in a velvet-lined pocket box. Holding this

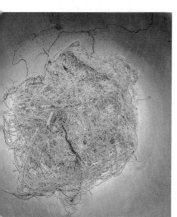

Cecilia's Threads

There are tiny mountain passes in Cecilia Hewett's pile of threads collected by un-picking her husband's old shirts.

Sculpture of K2 in rag

An avalanche is an awesome sight in snow and just as magnificent when it happens in a rag pile. Colours and textures with all their cultural associations, tumbling with ideas through the flux of deep time.

Textiles were invented in a pre-ceramic age, so we are talking about a seriously ancient technology which has moved human beings forward. The invention of machinery has not changed the craft that much. If you have practiced any of the simple methods of weaving, looping, braiding, knitting or crochet, then you are directly connected to early mankind.

Hesitation to cut or rip something is normal. Our minds tend to want familiar things to stay the same. The fold-out chart in this book provides support in strengthening your intention to deconstruct and reconstruct problematic textiles which are not fully serving you anymore. (Destroying other people's clothes against their wishes can be tempting, but is not encouraged here.)

The *Rag Manifesto* wants us to grow through craft. It has certainly helped me do that. Craft teachers know that people's creative urges arrive with varying forces. Based on my experience of running Rag School, the following diagrams are hints as to how and why we might start something.

Let's imagine that we want to cut up a problematic piece of clothing or soft furnishing. Most of the clothes I chop are worn beyond charity-shop quality. Sometimes I will cut up something new that I feel is badly designed, or which has been discarded rudely in a public place. Commonplace thinking could question your reasons for chopping up clothes that have wear left in them. I would argue that if the regeneration of a problematic piece of clothing is part of your personal development, creative joy and nurturing of an environment, then the practice is totally justified – unless the piece is of museum quality, in which case please halt the scissors. The story you create through the process of regeneration has value in itself. You are creating refugia.

Refugia are a part of the world which is being repopulated. Botanists might class a crevice in a barren landscape as a refugium, and study it to see how things might regenerate.

Refugia can also be taking refuge in your practice. It is a place where you can gather together all the craft skills you know, or are yet to find, and use them to re-populate your world. In refugia, you can abolish any form of horrific certainty; the safety of refugia allows for the most natural methods of development which can contain both magic and peace. Refugia should always be looked at from the point of the future. Refuge, like rag, is an in-between state, a place where we can bring certain things into view and imagine new pathways. This activity could be classed as therapy, but I urge you to think of it beyond that. Refugia is a necessity and your inquiry and experiments have what Kate Fletcher and Mathilda Tham, professors in design, termed in their 2019 Fashion Action Research Plan an 'Earth Logic' value which cannot be quantified by the current economic value systems of textile commerce.

rag manifesto

House Clearance

The detritus of life

'Detritus, n: An accumulation of debris of any sort.'
Oxford English Dictionary

hile I was writing this book, I was also clearing out my in-laws' home of 50 years. Rags have been collected there since the early 1970s, curated with a fascinating mixture of passions.

The house has had some happy times. The record collection describes a life of fun, hippy hope and an enjoyment of altered states. Something started to shift in the 1980s and the records ceased to be played. Life became difficult and somehow, through various traumas, there developed a security in never throwing anything away.

My in-laws were of Armenian refugee heritage and Metzmama was a clever and practical person; she made some beautiful clothes, carried out intricate mends and had the skills, if not the energy, to fix her many broken zips. Drawer after drawer contained hints at fun adventures, educational activities and aspirational dreams.

The darker side was the evidence of decay, particularly within the fabrics. Lying in drawers for years, these pieces of storied clothing now offer a space of contemplation, and even the possibility of poetry.

My mother-in-law knew that I liked working with rag. She also knew I would be the sole heir to her collection. I sensed an unspoken trust, sometimes shot at me through a clearly intentional wink as I commented on her eccentric gardening clothes. She always said her materials were her riches. In her lifetime she gave me a few sheets and duvet covers, but she would never let me touch the avalanches of fabrics, even if they were blocking the corridor or filling up the chair I wanted to sit on.

Metzmama must have loved the idea of leaving the political constraints of the former Soviet Union and coming to live in the freedom of the West, and in particular the land from which the Beatles came. The hostility and hardship she found gradually

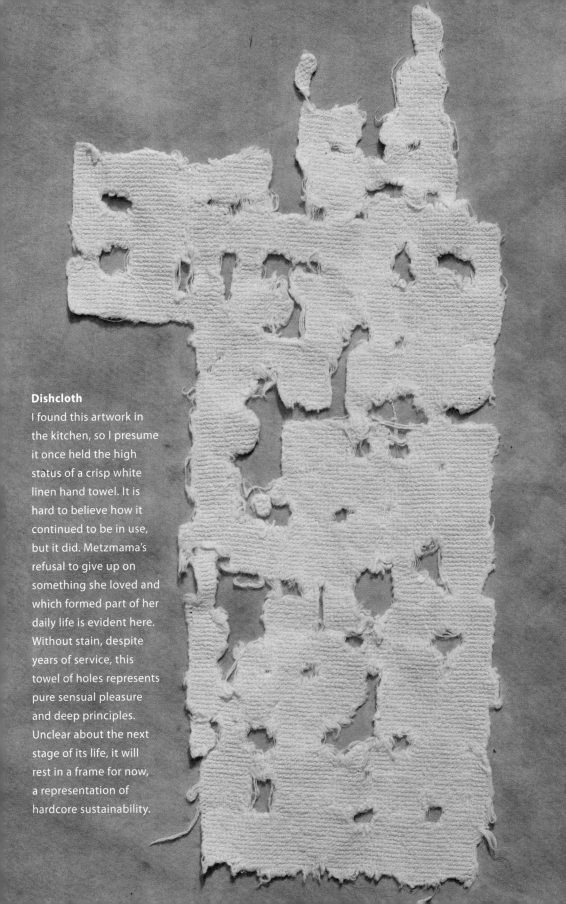

Dishcloth

I found this artwork in the kitchen, so I presume it once held the high status of a crisp white linen hand towel. It is hard to believe how it continued to be in use, but it did. Metzmama's refusal to give up on something she loved and which formed part of her daily life is evident here. Without stain, despite years of service, this towel of holes represents pure sensual pleasure and deep principles. Unclear about the next stage of its life, it will rest in a frame for now, a representation of hardcore sustainability.

Long johns
My father-in-law's dowry
of two kilos of gorgeously
soft thermal pant yarn,
collected over 40 years,
was put through a natural
indigo dye bath.

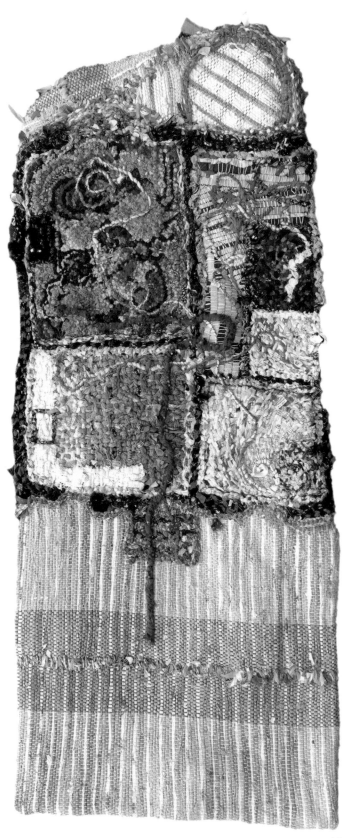

Floor Plan House Rug

The floor plan of Metzmama's house, made with the rags from her house using plaiting, weaving, hooky, kumihimo and plain weave. Living room, proddy on hessian with kumihimo walls; kitchen woven rag cord; bathroom and WC circular braiding; hallway off-loom weaving; outside areas plain weave; architectural details drawn in plait.

changed her mind. The telepathic instruction I receive from Metzmama is to use creative intelligence to give materials a further function, if only to prove her theories that neither communism nor capitalism work.

The challenge of clearing her house has made me realise that my husband Antranig and I were born of an era of progress. In order to continue on upwards trajectories, we have been encouraged to ditch the crap and streamline. My mother-in-law had a different idea and chose to save every odd sock and disintegrating wash cloth she had acquired since she arrived in England. This rag pile has been a spanner in the works of her progress, but I can't fault it. Metzmama's first love was nature and the rag pile demonstrates the natural, authentic order of an eccentric mind.

Hoarding is commonly seen as a symptom of mental illness, but I argue against that in Metzmama's case. This epicentre reflects what she saw around her, a paralytic fear of change, mixed with the feeling of scarcity created by capitalism. Wisely, Metzmama didn't trust the British waste collection services. What she needed for her personal growth was a creative community, providing a sensible system to process her collected materials, just as nature would intend. Antranig and I constantly question how progress can work in harmony with nature. We have to treat this tidy-up as a complex emotional and intellectual challenge.

Lose your rag

In the North of England, where I come from, there is a curious expression to 'lose your rag'. Closely related to the expression to 'let rip', it describes a point of heightened emotion where you wind up and explode. It is commonly thought of as being fuelled by anger, but it can also be silly and wild with joy and is always transformational. 'Lose your rag' also gave rise to Rag Week, the time designed for new arrivals at university to do activities which tip them over the edge into a deeper revealing of character. Chased by an old wet rag you should really start screaming.

My in-laws were continually losing their rags, teasing and provoking each other. As a guarded English person, I was always amazed to witness their heated arguments which led to collapses of laughter.

Clearing out my father-in-law's clothes, I was surprised to find 40 years' worth of thermal underwear in various states, some of them not too decent. The state of a man's pants is not something we generally like to read or talk about. I want to appear to you as a nice person, polite and finding my inspiration from spirit and nature, but my father-in-law's pants became an artwork, so pants it is. My husband found it painful to watch, so I chopped them into yarn at the end of the garden. The bad bits went on the compost heap and the yards of yarn from the rest

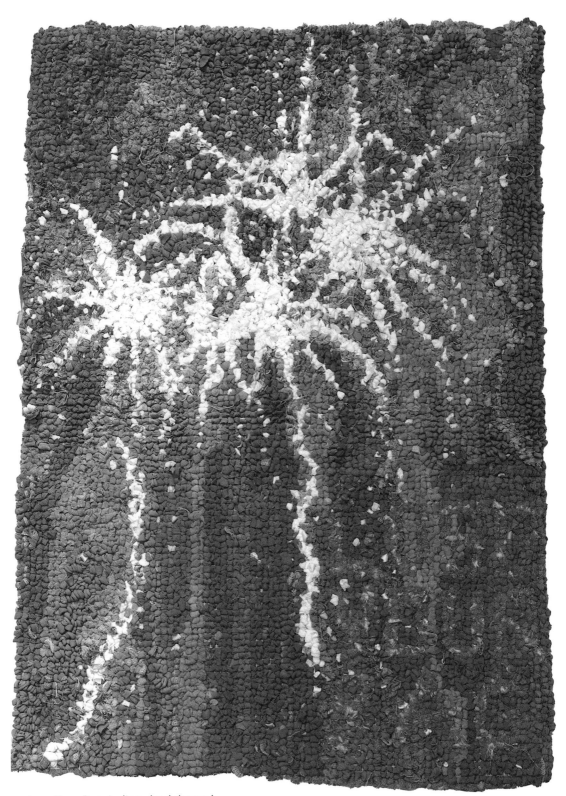

Lose Your Rag Indigo-dyed thermal
underwear and bedroom curtain, fancy
knickers and bed socks on canvas.

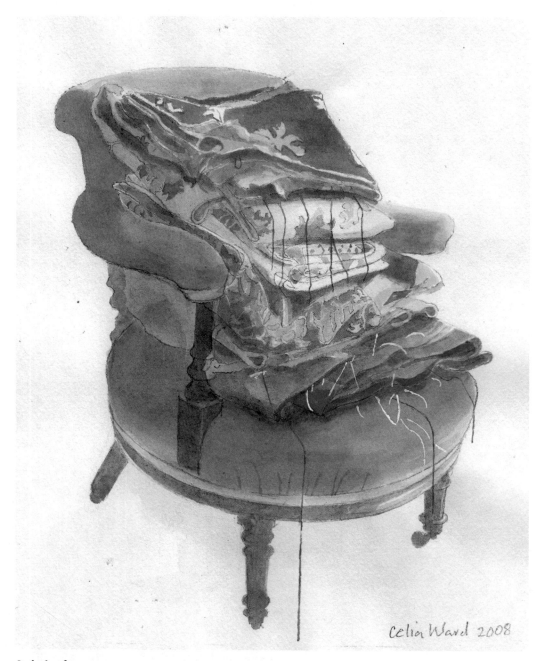

Celia Ward 2008

A chair of treasures

The rag pile at my
in-laws' house is not
photogenic, or useful
to show you. This
watercolour painting
by my friend, Celia

Ward articulates my
approach to house
clearance and takes
my defence of
Metzmama's mess
a stage further.

gained new life in a natural indigo bath. Indigo dye is a spiritual antiseptic for indecent cloth, an organic compound made from leaves that are broken down through a process of fermentation and composting. The vat becomes a living organism that needs to be constantly nurtured. While it is alive, it heals tired textiles by turning them magical and unpredictable blues, shades unachievable with synthetic dyes. As the cloth is pulled from the vat, it appears green until exposure to the air oxidizes the dye and turns it blue. Each time the cloth is dipped and exposed to the air; the shade of blue gets deeper. Indigo dying is a wonderful accompaniment to blue-sky thinking.

Clearing out my mother-in-law's underwear drawer, I found a completely different situation. Folded here were beautifully designed knickers which she had never really worn. It would be wrong to speculate why that was, but the vibe around the shiny lace was lovely, optimistic and not thrifty at all.

My response was a proddy firework display using both sets of pants, exploding with all the wildness of their kooky relationship (p71). Metzmama's beauty sparkling with a bang as it explodes with the stars combined with her husband's depth of intellect acting as a backdrop, merging with space. Pink bed socks shouting instruction.

I designed this piece to help tell the story of these people's amazing life and relationship, but I also wanted to dispel the myth of taboo materials and prove that loved ones need leave nothing untoward behind.

Once we cleared the stuff out of the house, we were able to see its structure more clearly. Here is a plan of the house (p69) made from the fabrics that were left behind. It is a piece about prompting memory and not dictating what is kept and what gets forgotten. Colours from the rooms are repeated in the clothes, which I suspect might be a common trait for most homeowners. The rug is not true to how the house is, but it is true to its character. The movements that were made around the house and the way it was lived in were sometimes different from the architect's original intention.

Storytime on Celia's chair

Celia is the founder of East London Textile Arts, where I run the Rag School (see p34). The painting represents Celia's mother's bedroom chair, with a neat pile of fabrics folded on the seat. When I first asked Celia about it, her response was 'Don't we all have a chair with fabric piled on it?'

For Celia, the drawing is like the story of *The Princess and the Pea*, a fairy tale by Hans Christian Andersen about a young woman whose royal ancestry is established by a test of her sensitivity; she couldn't sleep because a small pea hidden under many mattresses felt unbearably uncomfortable.

The story is a wonderful metaphor for our community project, teaching us not to judge people based on their appearance or circumstance, and regarding everyone as possible royalty. Textile waste on the streets of our city represents a pea under the mattress which stops us sleeping. Visit our workshop and we might appear to be at peace in our therapeutic craft worlds, but we are all working something out.

Celia knows from years of grass roots experience that it doesn't matter what the quality of your life, your home, or furniture is; if you are blessed with textile creativity, you will find a way to hoard material, put it to good use and learn something new. The peaceful, tidy intention of the fabrics on Celia's mother's chair set a precedent, showing there is strength in this home.

Fabrics in waiting are testimony to a practical outlook on life, with a loving respect for the order of creativity. Knowledge is power and this chair is a throne, dignified in accommodating a family and its abundance through the passage of time.

There is another fairy tale that we can use in our rag manifesto too. It is the story of King Midas. 4,000 years ago, or thereabouts, King Midas was sitting on his throne in Pessinus, a city of Phrygia, Lydia, somewhere in what is now Asian Turkey, when a drunken old school master was brought to him. Midas recognised him and treated him very well, entertaining him for ten days and nights. In return, the school master delighted King Midas and his court with stories and songs. On the eleventh day, King Midas sent the wayward school master back to his folks, who were so grateful for his generous hospitality, that they offered him any reward he wished for.

Midas asked that whatever he might touch should be changed into gold. The wish was duly granted and King Midas was delighted with his new power. Crazed, and dancing around his palace gardens, he leapt at every twig, leaf and rose, proudly turning them to gold in the morning sunshine. Working up an appetite with this extraordinary new ability, he ordered his servants to set a feast for lunch, whereupon he realized he could turn the food and drink to gold as well.

Pretty soon, King Midas realised he was in trouble. He couldn't eat and drink gold and his daughters complained that he had ruined the garden and the roses no longer had any scent. As the classical Roman poet Claudian states in his work '*In Rufinium*', 'He understood that his gift was a bane and in his loathing for gold, cursed his prayer.'

Today, King Midas and his golden finger are still causing havoc. Tired and on the lookout for cheap tricks, fast fashion makes us feel we have struck gold for a while. But we can play Midas at his own game. We can turn rags into riches.

rag manifesto

Hidden History

Two Cats by the Fire

Winifred Nicholson, courtesy of the Trustees of Winifred Nicholson. In the 1920s when Jovan's grandparents were living in Cumberland, they designed rugs and had them made by the Warwick family in the neighbouring farm. Rag rugging was traditional in Cumbria, but the pre-printed designs could be unimaginative. Ben and Winifred also knew Pablo Picasso who, like them, was pushing the boundaries of fine art with an interest in the naive and the reclaiming of materials. Both were interested in so-called primitive, or naive, art, and Ben in particular was stimulated by meeting Alfred Wallis.

painting, covering many genres of art – Popularist, Expressionist, Classical, Folk, Protest. It seems every home has a good idea, expressing the circle of life through the multiple histories layered within their domestic materials.

Using rag as a painterly medium to be worked with a community was an idea Ben and Winifred were familiar with. In the 1920s, Ben's father, the painter William Nicholson, and his wife, designed *The Signs of the Zodiac* for their local Women's Institute to make. The piece is now held in the Victoria and Albert Museum's (V&A) collection (see p77). We don't know much about how it came about, or for where it was destined for, but the subject of the zodiac is a clever idea for communal chat.

When I searched the V&A database for 'William Nicholson rag rug', I drew a blank. I finally found *Signs of the Zodiac* by searching for it by name and discovered that, rather than being described as a rag rug, this piece is captioned 'looped ribbon on canvas'. William Nicholson was a revered artist of course; rag rugging was for crafters.

It is interesting that we have so many regional words for what is commonly known as 'rag rug' – from proddy to looped ribbon on canvas – but none of them fit my personal view of rag rugging as a radical and versatile medium. When I asked Jovan about my elitist worry about labels he said, 'We're stuck with

"rag rug" I'm afraid, though the Americans call them hooked rugs.'

Jovan is right; these words don't matter at all. Mary Bewick was a farmer's daughter who lived next door to the Nicholsons in Banks Head and later married a farmer living in the remote Bewcastle area of Cumberland. Her rag rugs, *Sheep* and *Galloway Bull* are evidence of a deep-rooted knowledge of landscape and animals. The contours of the looped threads could only be made by someone who has spent their entire life caring for and observing animals. An intangible cultural heritage is clearly voiced through these large pieces. *Galloway Bull* and *Sheep* are examples of a very fine art which cannot be taught at art school. The cultural value of rag is irrelevant to genius and collaborative intelligence (or 'scenius' as Brian Eno termed it).

For a set of very confusing reasons, the art world has not been able to class rag rugs as 'art' and, as a result, they are rarely found in major museum collections. I find that disappointing, but Jovan's sparkle at the mention of this controversy gives me hope.

Soon a 'rag rug' will cease to be dusty, poor woman's work. Creative uprisings cannot be suppressed and, just as the snowdrops defy the cold weather and arrive 'unbidden', as Wordsworth put it in his poem, so our work doesn't think twice about gate crashing the art world party.

Farmyard

Designed by Jovan Nicholson, made by Florence Williams (87 x 95 cm, Private Collection).

From the 1960s onwards, Winifred was energized by a scene of young artists and focused deeply on designing rag rugs, many of which are sadly unaccounted for today. As a young boy Jovan and his brother, along with other grandchildren and some great nieces, were paid £1 to design a rug which was then made up for them. Winifred was clever to show the modern nature of a child's naive drawing.

Cat
Made by Elena and
Bertram Nicholson
depicting the family cat
who lived to be 20 years
old (45 x 48cm).

Birds over Yellow Fields,
2023 (46 x 46cm).
Louisa Creed is a niece of
Ben Nicholson and was
inspired by discovering
Winifred's textile work.
Louisa has been making
beautiful landscapes in
rag since 1988 and can
magically make the
weather change with her
sensitive handling of
colour and texture. Her
book *My Rag Rug Life* is
published by Rylett Press.

Materials

Materials, samples + techniques

'...Only the finale in the long sequence of operations from matter to product is left to us. We merely toast the bread. No need to get our hands into the dough.'

Anni Albers, *On Weaving*

It is important to remember that you don't need to buy much stuff to get on with rag work – find a good pair of scissors, start braiding with your fingers and work your way up to simple weaving tools, which you can buy second hand, or make yourself. The most important thing is discovering what you already know and have, and that costs nothing at all. That said, there are some things you might find useful.

Materials

The local charity shop is a magical material supply store. Artificial intelligence could never predict the serendipity with which textiles emerge from the jumble. Ecstatic combinations of found colour and texture might remind you of something interesting that you can elaborate on. Indications of new colour investigations are very healthy – it is all too easy to get stuck in familiar colour choices, and the cheapness of rag offers a safe space in which to experiment. There is a life-affirming enchantment in learning to accept the things we find and forget the things we were looking for. I repeatedly sense that the fabrics I find in weird places are waiting to offer support at a certain moment. You are on the right track when stuff you thought you hated surprises you by becoming the thing you want.

Pants and more pants

It could be unbearable to think about how many used pants there are strewn around the world. (Odd socks are much easier to talk about – and I do below.) All the best pants wear out, and are problematic to mend. Waste on pants includes decorative elastic, expanses of soft cotton and, in the case of thermal long pants, or long johns, a lot of spare fabric. Cut out the crotch area

Monroe Socks

My brother has travelled the world, climbed all of the Scottish Monroe mountains and has run around looking after difficult children in his job as a social worker. Here are some of his worn-out socks, cut into a clue. Obviously, my brother wore these socks for activities other than climbing mountains, but I think it is fair to say that the total weight of sock for that era of his life is 689g.

and dispose of it in whichever way you see fit. Cut the long legs, torso tubes or fancy waistband of underwear using the spiral cut method. On YouTube you can look up how to cut a bag into one continuous thread using this method. It is quite easy once you get your head around it.

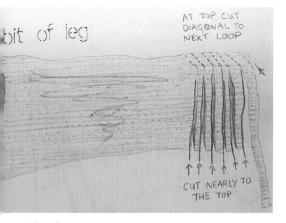

Chopleg

How to cut up a circular tube, such as a leg or arm, in one long thread to minimise joins.

Focus on socks

If you worry about being destructive and chopping something up, then an old sock is a good place to start. Many socks end up odd because people's lives are too busy to keep track of them. I asked a search engine to find out how many socks there are in the world and a person called Kevin kindly suggested that the answer is 98765435678876558876546788765367687786543546768764533546576756434435467875435 46. Discussing socks is the most glorious small talk and yet it is fascinating too, so ask a friend if they have any to donate.

When I started the Rag School with ELTA, one of the first participants to knock on the door was Emma Mathews of Socko. Socko is a sustainable sock brand which has produced the UK's first completely recycled and British-made sock. This was not an easy mission. Emma came to Rag School because

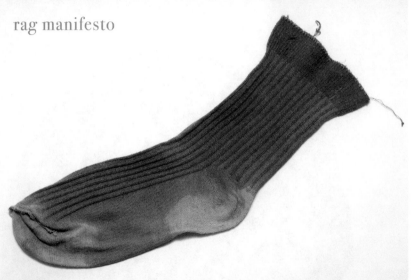

70s sock

This 100% synthetic well-worn odd sock was originally dark blue. Initially, had super-tight elastic around the ribbed cuff, which corroded over time to become mysteriously baggy. It is unclear whether the strengthening thread was meant to be pink. This non-biodegradable design is a rare sight these days, suggesting that the partner of this sock, and its siblings from the factory, must be deep in landfill. It remains as a reminder of many small things.

she had built up textile waste in the process of producing socks and wanted some time out to be creative with friends and figure out what to do with it. The waste was mostly small loops which are made at the toe closing machine. The waste from Socko's first collection produced one amazing weave on a peg loom (see p91).

As we wondered over the effect, Emma explained that her sock waste was just a small part of an enormous mountain of sock toe loops, and she invited me to visit the factory.

On our journey north, I tried to extract from Emma just how much love and determination she puts into her sock business. Socko is an intentionally small-scale business and,

in a few action-packed years, Emma has discovered there are all kinds of interesting complications to be had within ethical sock manufacture. Emma's fascination with the project is the craftsmanship which goes into every stage of the product.

There is a lot that can go wrong. Dropped stitches, wrongly set elastic on a cuff, irregular colour mixing, and mistakes setting the gauge or tension, all result in socks that cannot be sold and end up in the waste. Getting the tension wrong, for example, can result in a sock that's a metre and half long with a size 20 foot! Understanding the difficulties in sock manufacture made me appreciate socks in a whole new way. Factory waste can be beautiful and teach you a lot.

Sock Hell
Carding socks at the entrance to hell. Waste from Socko on an image from Cassell's Dore Gallery, engraving of Dante's Inferno, c1890.

Ball of sock waste in 2 ply
The sock waste has a small amount of merino fleece added to hold the lumpy bits together.

Carders with sock waste
To card, put the handles of the carders opposite to each other, connect the two sets of teeth, and pull the teeth apart horizontally. Enjoy this work with a straight back and working with your upper chest muscles.

Socko sock waste 'Shoulder Boulder,' pictured on the front cover, was made largely from these loops, woven on a bespoke loom.

Sock mats

Above: Emma Mathews' Socko mat, woven from the sock loops of her first sock collection. Made on a peg loom.
Right: Socko Crash Mat made out of the long sock trails rejected in the process of setting up the knitting machine. Gathered on a trip to the factory.

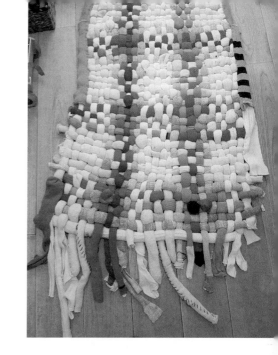

Braiding in the round

- Take a number of rag strips – I recommend five to start with – and choose whether you like to work from left to right or right to left. (This description is left to right.)
- Take the thread on the left and work it over, under, over, under the next four threads. You will end up with a new thread on the left. Take this new thread and repeat the over, under method.

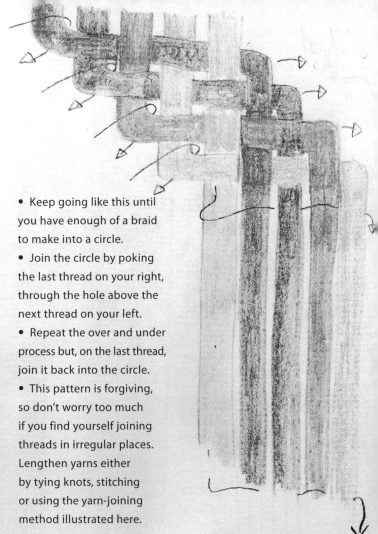

- Keep going like this until you have enough of a braid to make into a circle.
- Join the circle by poking the last thread on your right, through the hole above the next thread on your left.
- Repeat the over and under process but, on the last thread, join it back into the circle.
- This pattern is forgiving, so don't worry too much if you find yourself joining threads in irregular places. Lengthen yarns either by tying knots, stitching or using the yarn-joining method illustrated here.

Yarn joining method

Avoid lumpy knots with this easy way to join rag yarn. Cut a slice in the ends of two pieces of rag yarn you want to join – let's call them 'A' and 'B'. Pass the end of A through the end of B, then pass the other end of A through its own slot. Gently pull tight.

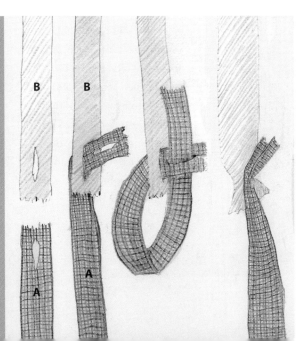

Hooky

The basic concept of hooky is to hold the yarn underneath the canvas, poke the hook in where you want to make a loop, grab the yarn with the hook and pull it through. Make the loop the length you want, but be consistent. From here on, you just go wherever you like. It takes a while to get your speed up and knitted fabrics are easier to use. You don't need to work in rows like tapestry; instead you can move around as if you were brushing paint. If you change your mind about a mark, it is very simple to undo.

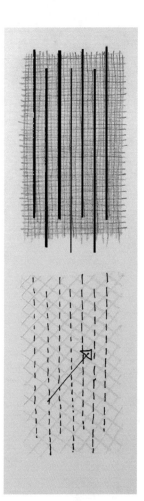

Grain / bias

All woven fabrics have what is called a 'grain'. This refers to the vertical warp threads and the horizontal weft threads. If you tug a fabric along its grain, either lengthways or widthways, it will have quite a tough tension. If you tug the fabric at 45 degrees to the grain, you will notice the fabric gets stretchy. This is called the 'bias' and it can be used to make wonderful curves. Cutting rag yarns on the bias is time consuming, but it can make lovely effects for braiding. Ripping only happens along a normal grain.

Bias binding makers

You can make your rag strips by cutting with pinking shears to minimise fraying. If you are into neat lines which bend perfectly, get yourself a set of bias binding makers and spend hours with a hot steam iron, inhaling the loveliness of hot fabric, folding in the edges and making the best rag yarn possible. It's even better cut with pinking shears. You get out what you put in with a practice like this.

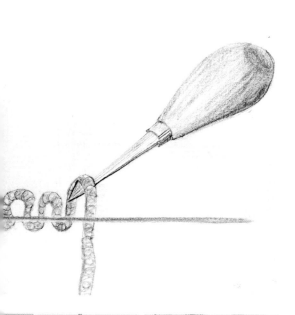

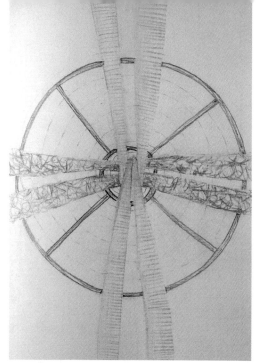

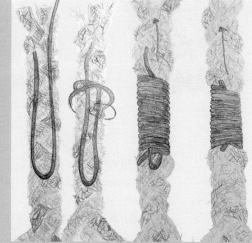

Whipping and tassels

Whipping is a rare craft with multiple uses. Generally, it provides the punctuation at the end of a piece of cord, rope or plait, stopping the unravelling of something plied. At ELTA we made big, whipped handles on our skipping ropes. Decorative whipping on passementerie tassels provides the opportunity for a lifetime's work, getting your binding really tight and super neat.

Kumihimo braiding

Japanese braiding is mind-bogglingly clever and not too hard to pick up. Traditionally, braid is made with eight fine threads, passed over a round frame in differing mathematical sequences under even tension provided by beautiful handmade bobbins. In ancient Japanese culture you will find these beautiful braids tying up scrolls, or used as belts for Samurai swords. The neatness they represent goes way beyond the actual braid.

Rag School's skipping rope braids were based on the teachings of Kumihimo braiding, but adapted for impatient punks who are happy to sit with an old lampshade as a base, adding tension to their threads with rocks, and enjoying the unexpected results of irregular materials.

Samples

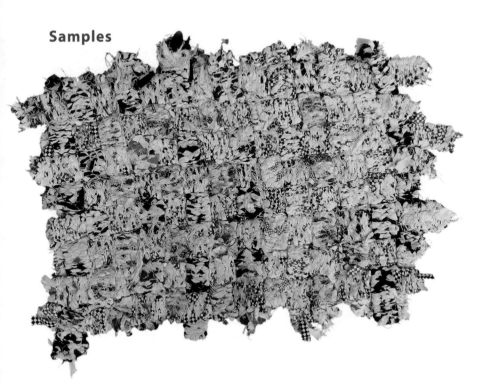

Black and White Rubble

(Welsh weaving sticks)
When my husband moved
into his student digs, the once
white curtains in his room
were pretty tatty. Twenty
years later, when I met him,
they were still hanging there.
One day I took them down
to see if they would launder.
I could see they had been
a fresh vision in the 1950s
– a new sort of material,
textured on one side, shiny
on the other. Of course, they

ripped to shreds, but in their
newfound freedom as a large
pile of detritus, they wove
together beautifully with
other, smaller, pieces of aged
black and white materials
forming a textile that almost
had the dense feel of
compressed rubble. This
carpet is woven on Welsh
weaving sticks. I created many
strips of weave and then wove
the strips together.

Made in Italy

There are unthinkable
amounts of homeless
selvedge edging in the world,
edges binned once the
garment pieces have been
cut. The edge which made
this rug was from a pure wool,
Italian cloth. The selvedge
had a tough quality, perhaps
as a result of being worked
with a white linen to aid the
cloth as it rolled through the
finishing machines and
created this snazzy label.
As I was weaving off loom,
I had to tack the rag yarn in
place as it kept wanting to
do something else.

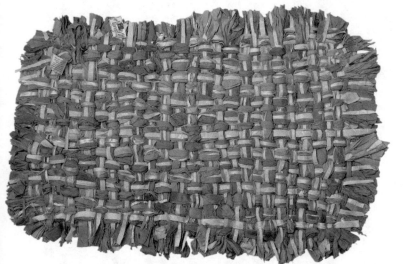

Sidestrike Mat

This mat was made from
a collection of sun-damaged
curtain linings which didn't
have the strength to hold a
seam anymore. Bunched up
into a really thick yarn, woven
and embellished with some
more modern rags, I suspect
that if this mat could be
employed as a bedside mat,
it could easily outlive me.

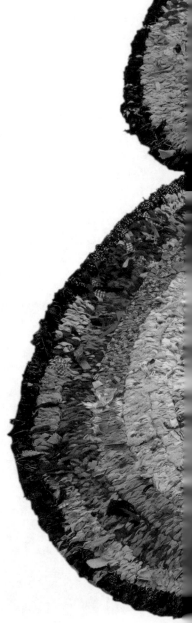

'2, 4, 6, 8'
I made this on a residency at The Experimental Weave Lab at the Clothworkers' Company in the heart of the City of London. It was midsummer and I was thinking about ancient migrations towards stone circles, and how the stones would have been decorated with luminous patterns depicting vibrations and journeying. The sticks were wonderfully portable and I would walk around town, weaving as I went. '2, 4, 6, 8' was the natural number sequence of the circles and rings as they emerged through an abstract idea about motherhood.

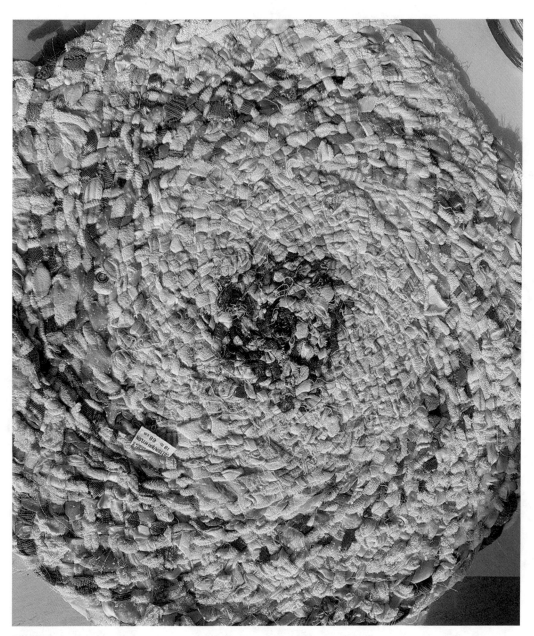

Braiding in the round

Braiding in the round (see p99)
with the colours found in
Metzmama's bathroom.

Labyrinth of
a creative mind

The labyrinth has no dead ends

'He who binds to himself a joy/ Does the winged life destroy;
He who kisses the joy as it flies/ Lives in eternity's sunrise.'

Eternity, William Blake

I love writing, but really I prefer an artwork to stand alone without a written explanation. The contemporary art world has developed into quite a wordy place, where clever jargon instructs us to think hard about what we can understand intuitively by looking. There is nothing wrong with that – I enjoy getting my head around challenging concepts – but the glorious absence of words in art summons us to journey in a fashion that is more extraordinary than an instructed one.

Textiles provide an immediate entrance to that track, drawing us in to see, feel and shift ourselves with pure intuition. Yarns often hook me up to deep memories that I don't need to verbalize. Awareness and imagination are active and robust sources, not always validated by our wordy education systems.

Journeys I take through my rag habit often introduce me to ancestral beings or future situations. The physical nature of the work itself helps me to feel the weight I give to the earth, here and now. If we lose touch with the earth, due to the superficial times we are encouraged to live in with their taboo over the use of trashed materials, the rag pile becomes an alternative space to open our heads, a doorway into abundance of thought, everyday art and protest. Perhaps in some instances, rag could be the only material to offer us a way out of the conundrum of the Anthropocene.

Labyrinth Circular braid.

Fire
Sometimes the mess of fibres
that gathers on the studio floor
can ignite a new idea.

High-vis rock

This was woven directly onto a rock while being driven down the motorway. Multi-billion-pound transport projects spit out luminous twills and knits with glass-reflective ribbons. Some of these garments are very big, with poppered pockets and chunky zips. They rest on railings, sleep in shrubs, or lie in the road or on railway sidings. The strange thing is, if you put these garments on, you can become invisible. The earth squeezed out some unbelievable dye stuffs to make these garments. If you wore high-vis on a medieval construction site, the workforce would have gone crazy thinking these were garments from heaven, or the underworld. Put one on and you might have danced your heart out around a rock like this one.

Below: Overalls

In lockdown a builder left a boiler suit in a skip on our road. On further inspection I realised that the zip had broken. With rubber gloves on, I lifted it home and put it through a 90-degree wash. The design was made to match a famous brand of work tools, and was mostly black with grey highlights and the odd fluorescent orange flash. I added some extra black to this weave but essentially it is the boiler suit cut directly into yarn and woven on a Brinkley loom.

Left: Measuring tabards on the road

In the old days, I used to measure materials in yards and metres. Collecting high-vis workwear from the street, I discovered I have several bags full of the same sort of material all cut into strange shapes. There is a lot to work with, but how much have I got? My studio is not big enough to lay it all out, so I used the street. Here is confirmation that I have almost two car lengths worth of high vis. This information is vital in knowing what it is possible to make. Re-programming the creative mind is an important part of Rag School. Could the domestic industry of the future measure textile quantities using standard car-parking measurements?

Credits

Rag School participants
Prof. Diane Haigh
Richard McVetis
Celia Pym
Hannah Coulson
Celia Ward
Sonia Tuttiet
Lucy Gunning
Alison Richmond
Bobbie Kociejowski
Lorna Hamilton Brown
Simon Jackson
Lucky Lowe
Prof. Elizabeth Stade
Nurse Annie
Studio Brieditis & Evans
Prof. Prue Bramwell Davis
Jovan Nicholson
Clare Lynch
Sindy Jackson
Prue Guthrie
Natalie Silk
Emma Mathews (Socko)
Phillipa Brock
Elizabeth Ashdown
Rosa Parkes

Sallyanne Wood
Monica Grose Hodge
Mani
Laura Holland
Taskin
Sameena
Andrew Brown
Helen
Jemima
Magnus
Athena Lax
Cassian Lax
Lizzie Children
Bingham Basman
Nick Stade
Iona Ramsay
Sophia Ramsay
James Ramsay
Celia Ward
Sonia Tuttiet
Sandra
Amy Twigger Holroyd
Paul Powlesland
Ryan Powell
Lola the dog
Lucy Gunning

Donations of textile waste
Bella Freud bellafreud.com
Hairy Mary hairymary.co.uk
Socko socko.shop
Swift Hosiery jalexswift.co.uk
Yodomo yodomo.co
Berdjouhi and Michael Basman
Elspeth Dennison

Rag Manifesto production credits
Ruth Roxanne Board, studio photography
Andrew Brown, photography
Antranig Basman, photography
Raphael Appleby, research and inspiration
Cecilia Hewett, research and inspiration
Jovan Nicholson, research and inspiration
Louisa Creed, donation of rag rug image
Emma Matthews, Socko
Celia Ward, for directing Rag School at
East London Textile Arts
Katy Bevan who makes it all go.

This book was written for Antranig Basman.